The 10 Secrets to Great Rebound Control

By Ian Clark *with* Leo Luongo

Copyright © 2010
Ian Clark

All rights reserved. No part of this book may be reproduced, stored in a retrieval system, or transmitted in any form or by any means – electronic, mechanical, photocopying, recording, or otherwise – without the prior written permission from the author. The only exception is brief quotations in printed reviews.

Printed in the United States of America

ISBN 1-453-71542-8
EAN-13 978-1-453-71542-0

Credits:
Cover and book design by Rob Hicks
Photography by Jeff Vinnick, courtesy of Vancouver Canucks®

CONTENTS

PREFACE 7

INTRODUCTION 9

#1 – FUNDAMENTALS – KEY TO REBOUND CONTROL 13

#2 – DEVELOP A PUCK-COLLECTION HABIT 19

#3 – NARROW YOUR BUTTERFLY 23

#4 – PUSH AND STEER - DON'T KICK 29

#5 – HAVE A STICK-TO-PUCK MENTALITY 35

#6 – UNDERSTAND THE POWER OF SQUARE SAVES AND GEOMETRY 45

#7 – EXCEL IN THE EASY AREAS 51

#8 – REDUCE POST-SAVE DELAY 57

#9 – ACCEPT THE PUCK 63

#10 – DEVELOP REBOUND-CONTROL PRIDE 69

HONORABLE MENTION 73

CONCLUSION 75

BIOGRAPHIES 77

NEXT IN THE 10 SERIES 79

PREFACE

By Roberto Luongo

Ian Clark has coached and mentored me for more than half of my NHL career. During this time, he has uncovered countless details that help me to improve my game. Indeed, the very improvements that he, and my brother Leo, write about in this handbook are mechanics, tools and philosophies that I use daily to drive my game forward.

I was introduced to Ian in 2001 when he joined the Florida Panthers coaching staff. He and I stayed in close contact after he left Florida for Vancouver the very next season. Coincidentally, when my time ended in Florida with my trade to Vancouver, he and I were reunited. Small adjustments in my stance and depth positioning have allowed me to climb out of funks while innovative approaches and tactics that he brings each year help me to continue to push my game forward.

Ian provides support in all aspects of my game. From technical and tactical expertise to handling mental challenges that confront us all as a season unfolds. He is an invaluable resource as a coach, friend and mentor.

During summers, I have a number of instructional resources that I use to prepare for the upcoming season. In recent years, this has come to include my brother Leo who has become an intuitive goaltending coach with a unique perspective on the position. He has an outstanding knowledge of mechanics and, most importantly to me, has a great feel for the intangibles of the position. Mechanics are straightforward but his ability to identify other issues makes him an important part of my pre-season preparation.

I strongly recommend "The 10 Secrets to Great Rebound Control" to goaltenders at every level of play. These 10 tips will help you, as they help me, control more pucks and make your team more competitive. Sometimes the most powerful concepts are the easiest to implement. This handbook is an easy read and highlights simple improvements that you, yourself, can add to your game. It is an excellent resource for committed goalies, parents and coaches.

Good luck with your goaltending,

Roberto Luongo

INTRODUCTION

This second book in The 10 Series of Goaltending Handbooks is designed to be a technical support guide aimed at improving your rebound control. Each chapter provides a comprehensive look at a valuable rebound-control technique or concept.

Rebound control is truly one of the lost arts of goaltending. As goaltenders have migrated to a butterfly-style approach, rebound control has taken a back seat. The focus of development over the last 10-15 years has shifted starkly to a drop-and-block mentality with the intent to cover maximum space with wide and compact positions. There have been many positives during this recent generation of development. Certainly, it has spawned exceptional and widespread growth in basic fundamentals – specifically, goaltender movement and positioning.

Interestingly, the first chapter of this book, Fundamentals - Key to Rebound Control, points to the connection between fundamental improvement in a goalie's basic skill set and what should be a corresponding improvement in rebound control. Where the disconnection has occurred, however, is in the loss of reactivity associated with a drop-and-block mentality. As reactivity has declined so, too, has puck control.

The primary emphases of this book are twofold.

First, we want to refocus attention onto the rebound-control category of development. This is vital because the greatest volume of "grade A" scoring chances come from rebounds. Therefore, it can be argued that re-establishing a grasp on good puck control can have a significant performance return.

Roberto Luongo stays visually attached to the puck following his save, making retention and control easier.

The second emphasis is to take today's generation of goaltenders and provide a solid set of tools and techniques that will dovetail with the modern game to improve one's puck control. Given the dramatic and widespread change in the position, traditional rebound control techniques don't entirely mesh with the modern game. Here, we present a modern blueprint for exceptional puck control.

Leo and I have worked hard to condense the concepts of rebound-control into these 10 (plus honorable mentions) meaningful improvements. While there are many other intricacies associated with rebound control, this compilation will provide the greatest benefit in a simple, easy-to-read handbook. As with the first book, each chapter represents a straightforward improvement. Each improvement aims to enhance your puck-control game and is one that you can implement, largely, on your own.

Like anything in goaltender development, repetition, discipline and self-initiative are the keys to success. The improvements noted here, for the most part, require these three self-driven attributes. The improvements

Introduction

are not complex. They simply require your attention on a full-time basis. If you are disciplined, these things will become instinctive and habitual. They take little in the way of additional physical effort. Therefore, if you can accept the notion of "full-timing" these concepts, we can assure you that your puck-control game will improve and improve quickly. Falling into the "part-time" trap will limit the power of these concepts.

As you embark on this read, do not underestimate the power of our Honorable Mention list. While they have not made the "10" list, they have dramatic effects on performance as well. You should consider these a part of your broader list and all of these should form a part of your philosophical approach to rebound control, the position and your performance.

The 10 Secrets to Great Rebound Control

#1
FUNDAMENTALS – KEY TO REBOUND CONTROL

Understanding the relationship between a goaltender's fundamentals and success is crucial to development. The fundamentals of the position lead to performance success in every goaltender skill category, including rebound control. A goalie's fundamentals not only play a role but are indispensable in a goalie's performance quest.

A great first step is to understand The Goaltender Development Pyramid (see Figure 1). This concept shows the myriad of major skill groups underlined by the key fundamentals – skating, movement and positioning.

Let's walk through this skill progression to provide further clarity. As we do this, we will always start with the level above. For instance, when speaking about "basic skating", we will relate it to the tier above "position-specific movement".

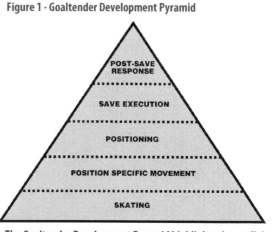

Figure 1 - Goaltender Development Pyramid

The Goaltender Development Pyramid highlights the goalie's fundamental skill groups and the progression that they follow from a developmental perspective. Each skill rung requires proficiency at the previous level.

For a goalie to move effectively in a confined space, the crease, the goalie requires the ability to start, stop, rotate and adjust rapidly in sometimes wider spaces and sometimes smaller spaces. This confined-space movement within the crease is called position-specific movement. In order to achieve these rapid edge movements with the skates, a goaltender must establish exceptional edge-control skills. This is the primary goal of basic skating.

When a player, or goalie, begins to skate, they learn to stride, stop, turn, crossover and pivot. These skills are all edge-driven moves. The old

Basic positioning, fueled by strong movement skills, is a precursor for good rebound control. Together, these fundamentals provide a calming and simplifying affect to a goalie's save process.

cliché "the goalie must be the best skater on the team" has some validity for this reason. Starting, stopping and turning in a very small space, like the crease, is far more complex than doing so on the larger ice surface. Therefore, it is safe to say that basic skating is the precursor to position-specific movement skills.

We can use this same logic as we climb the pyramid.

Let's now talk about positioning (the next level). A goalie's position is made up of three elements:

1. Angle
2. Depth
3. Body

These three positional concepts combine to place the goaltender around the net in an optimal place to make a save. The question is – how did they get to this position? The answer is simple – position-specific movement. Therefore, it is equally safe to say that a goalie's positioning hinges on the quality of their position-specific movement. Without the means to get to position efficiently and consistently, the goalie's positions will be impaired. Notice, again, that the rung above (in this case, positioning) is largely dependent on the quality of skill found on the level below (in this instance, position-specific movement).

Let's move on and discuss save execution. The simplicity of a goalie's save, naturally, is affected by the quality of the opposition's shot. More importantly, however, it is affected by the quality of the goalie's positioning. A goalie that combines angle, depth and body in a logical fashion for a given shot will occupy a large volume of "space". "Space", in goalie terms, is the triangular puck-net relationship (as indicated in Figure 2 on the next page). One can easily see that a goalie who positions well will reduce the complexity of their save by reducing the distance required to move to make that save. In examining the Fig. 2 illustration, imagine three goalie positions - on the goal line, in the middle of the crease and on top of the crease. As the lines emanating from the puck indicate, a well-positioned goalie does not need to move as far to make a save. Therefore, it is safe to say that the quality, and simplicity, of a goalie's save movement is directly proportionate to the quality of their positioning.

On the next rung of the pyramid lies rebound control and recovery. We can expect to find that quality rebound control and recovery capabilities will, in large part, hinge on the quality of the save execution, which hinged on positioning, which hinged on position-specific movement.

This all makes perfect sense. Let's go back to the

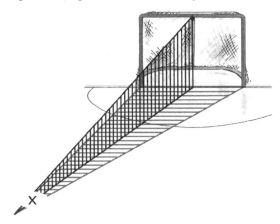

Figure 2 – Triangular Puck-Net Relationship

It is the puck-net relationship (illustrated here by the lines connecting the puck and the net) that a goaltender constantly strives to occupy. It is a goalie's positioning that determines the volume of basic coverage attained within this space.

discussion of save execution. We stated and the facts show that a well-positioned goaltender does not have to move as far to make a save. This is termed positionally efficient. A positionally-efficient goalie makes, on average, a shorter, more stable and controlled save than a positionally inefficient goaltender. As such, this shorter move means less time is used to respond to the puck and more time can be used to customize the save to include rebound control. Due to the less extended and less prone save position, a goalie's recovery sequence is easier to initiate. All told, both rebound control and recovery skills are enhanced by effective save execution.

Let's recap. Skating leads to improved movement. Movement leads to improved positioning. Positioning leads to improved save execution. Finally, a controlled save leads to improved rebound control and/or recovery.

These statements are unequivocal. The Goaltender Development Pyramid holds true. Success at each level requires success and aptitude at all previous levels meaning that there is a direct correlation between the quality of one's rebound control and the base fundamentals of the position.

#1 – Fundamentals – Key to Rebound Control

Regardless of your current level of play, the recognition of this relationship between fundamentals and rebound control is important because rebounds are important. This means that you can never turn a blind eye on the development and maintenance of these fundamental skill groups whether you are a beginner or an accomplished pro.

The 10 Secrets to Great Rebound Control

#2

DEVELOP A PUCK-COLLECTION HABIT

This is the only skill/habit that has made the first two books in The 10 Series of Goaltending Handbooks. Secondly, this is the only rebound-control item that made the first book. This all underscores the importance of this specific habit. It's not difficult and yet most goalies are prepared

The ability to collect and retain loose pucks is a powerful and simple concept that Luongo excels at. This ability takes little specific skill but rather is derived from discipline and commitment.

The 10 Secrets to Great Rebound Control

to ignore its significance. For readers of *The 10 Quickest Ways to Improve Your Game*, **don't skip this chapter**. Remember, repetition reigns supreme when trying to perfect either a skill or a habit. Furthermore, to coax you into giving this chapter your full attention, we have offered some additional insight on the topic.

As we stated in *The 10 Quickest Ways to Improve Your Game*, its purpose is to provide goaltenders and coaches with 10 meaningful ways to improve a goalie's game significantly but more importantly, quickly. This puck-collection habit may, actually, have the most immediate and direct impact on game success. By definition, we are talking about the action of collecting or gathering loose pucks after a save.

The reason that most goalies do not endeavor to collect ALL available pucks is because it seems trivial. One of the greatest goalies ever to play the game, Roberto Luongo, is a testament that opposes this "triviality" attitude. There is never a puck that is within gathering distance that Roberto does not draw into his possession. Interestingly, there are few goaltenders that have the rebound control that he does. Much of his puck control comes from this automatic collection habit.

There are many options when it comes to a loose puck:

1. Ignore it
2. Sweep it away
3. Follow it but don't collect it
4. Collect it sometimes but not others
5. Collect it always

Let's examine the pros and cons of these options.

In the first case, the goalie simply chooses to ignore it. There are a host of problems. Most significant is that if the goalie chooses to ignore it then it was impossible to be visually attached to the puck through the save process. They are unknowingly training their muscle memory to not refill space when these pucks are at the side. The opportunity to improve the speed and coordination of gathering in these pucks is lost. The ability to cover a loose puck is delayed due to the ignorance applied to the process. Finally, and most critically, is the fact that ONLY when the puck is in the goalie's possession can the goalie feel confident that the puck is not in the back of the net.

#2 – Develop a Puck-Collection Habit

In the second case, instead of collecting and gathering the puck in, the goalie is choosing, as a matter of habit, to sweep it or push it away and back into the play. First off, this is a habit in and of itself. This formed habit will transcend itself into their game. While the goalie may be moving the puck out of the current danger spot, there is no guarantee that it isn't ending up in another, or even worse, danger spot. The puck remains in play. Not only does the goalie not know who might get possession of the loose puck but also does not, ultimately, know if the puck will end up in the back of the net.

In the third case, the goalie follows the loose puck when it is off to one side or the other but does not actually draw it in and possess it. While the goalie is following the puck with both eyes and body, which is very important, there is a lost opportunity to retain and control the puck. Furthermore, the hand-eye coordination that can be established by gathering pucks that have come off the body or pads is tossed away.

The final negative approach is the part-time approach. Part-timing any activity does not establish habit. Habits are instinctive actions that have been created through tireless repetitions - good or bad. If you choose to cover one but not the next then you have zero growth. You should note that you do not get to take a "plus" for a good execution without taking a "negative" for a bad execution. Therefore, the part-timer who does everything kind of fifty/fifty never makes progress because they are always losing the benefit of their previous positive action.

Yes, this improvement is trivial. Its trivialness, however, is not in its importance but rather in how much effort it takes. The volume of effort required to gather a loose puck is the only thing trivial. Trivial by definition is small and inconsequential. Well, collecting a loose puck, from the perspective of effort, is trivial because the effort required is so tiny and so inconsequential to one's total effort that to not adopt this practice plainly states one's non-commitment.

Let's return to the concept of hand-eye coordination. In watching and training many elite hockey athletes, one of the true gifts of the superstars is hand-eye coordination. Sure there are many other attributes that these gifted athletes share but a common athletic thread is hand-eye coordination. Puck collection is one of the very best goaltender-specific hand-eye coordination exercises that one can execute. The eyes are being

The 10 Secrets to Great Rebound Control

trained to track the puck to and off the body and without hesitation the hands are triggered – one with a stick in support – to gather these pucks into the goalie's possession. The committed goalie with the countless repetitions available, in this regard, can separate themselves from their goaltending peers and also from opposition shooters. We cannot ever emphasize enough the power of this rebound-control habit and the absolute direct performance benefit you can receive. All of this can be achieved for nominal additional effort.

As we know, the goaltender plays the key role. The goaltender plays a leadership role. The goaltender has the single largest, individual impact on team success. To adopt these vital yet "trivial" habits is not an option for the responsible goaltender. This goalie recognizes their role and seeks out competitive advantages. As described at the beginning (and in the last handbook – *The 10 Quickest Ways to Improve Your Game*) – this one is a big one!

#3
NARROW YOUR BUTTERFLY

While rebounds are generated in many ways, the goaltender's pads create the most complex problem. Shots to the glove are easily controlled through catching. Shots to the body are easily controlled through cradling. Shots to the blocker are easily controlled by "cocking" and "rotating" the wrist. Shots to the stick are easily controlled due to the maneuverability of the stick. The pads represent an entirely different situation.

A narrowing of the butterfly provides increased leg maneuverability and improved geometrics that assist in rebound-control endeavors. Luongo is one of the few masters of a narrower butterfly position.

Pads can't catch, cradle, cock, rotate or do much in the way of maneuvering. They are large surfaces that are predetermined by the positioning of the legs. The legs themselves are not only larger and more cumbersome but also are responsible for the goalie's movement so they are often pre-occupied heading into a save.

With these complexities, however, there are things that can be done to drive improvements in pad control. The next four chapters will focus on rebound control with the pads. These topics include:

1. Narrow Your Butterfly (this chapter)
2. Push and Steer - Don't Kick
3. Have a Stick-to-Puck Mentality
4. Understand the Power of Square Saves and Geometry

The first thing to recognize is that you cannot eliminate rebounds off the pads. The focuses should be to, first, reduce these rebounds and, second, stop inflaming them. On this latter note, many goaltenders tend to inflame pucks off the pads for reasons soon to be covered.

Let's focus in on the topic of narrowing your butterfly. In essence, butterfly width, as it relates to rebound control, comes down to two things: geometry and maneuverability. The pad is essentially a long plane. Depending on the angle that we place this plane, we should not be surprised by the puck's behavior when hitting it.

Figure 1 highlights this point. We can see that from a purely geometric perspective the puck's behavior is highly predictable for a given puck trajectory.

Furthermore, as a

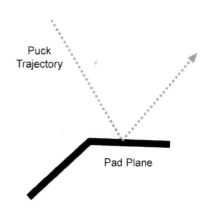

Figure 1 – Puck Trajectory

As the hard puck collides with another firm surface, it careens predictably. Basic geometric functions can be used to determine the precise nature of the rebounding puck.

3 – Narrow Your Butterfly

goaltender's butterfly widens, the maneuverability of the legs is reduced. At a goalie's maximum width (which is different for each goaltender based upon anatomy and equipment), the maneuverability of the legs is lost making the butterfly plane fixed along with the puck trajectory off of this now fixed plane.

A narrowing of the butterfly has a number of performance benefits, which we will review to support the narrowing process, but certainly the pre-eminent advantage is improved rebound control. Specific to our rebound-control discussion these improvements include the recapturing of leg maneuverability and improved geometrics. Our first task will be to break down these rebound-control features before briefly reviewing additional benefits of a narrowing of the butterfly.

Figure 2 – Butterfly Width

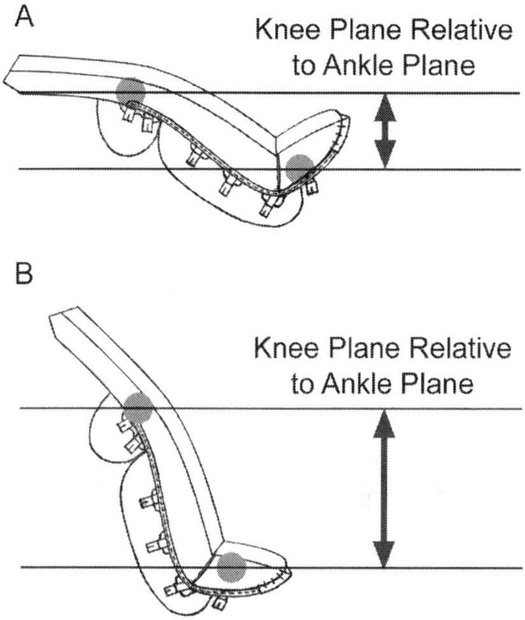

A goalie's butterfly width is determined by how close the ankle plane is to the knee plane.

IMPORTANT: Notice that the term "narrowing" has been used. This is important. We are not saying that a butterfly has to be narrow. We do not advocate for a specifically narrow or a specifically wide butterfly but rather a versatile butterfly width. Goalies should have a range to their butterfly width – in some cases, maximum coverage is important (e.g. a screen with lost vision) and in other cases a narrower position has benefits (e.g. a bad-angle shot). Lastly, a body position that eliminates all maneuverability will always have a negative performance impact.

SIMPLE GEOMETRY

There are two basic geometry lessons here. One is relative to butterfly width and one is relative to the angle of access into the net.

First, when it comes to the butterfly, the closer the ankles are to the plane of the knees (see Figure 2A on the previous page), the wider the goaltender's butterfly. Of course, it is impossible for the ankles to be past the knees and, virtually impossible, for them to be on the same plane. Due to our knowledge of geometry, we can state that the closer the ankles are to the knee plane (i.e. the wider the butterfly), the greater the number of rebounds. Since they cannot be on the same plane, the pads are not square to the puck which further inflames the rebound because it makes it careen off-square to the goalie. The consequence of an off-square shift in puck position is that the goalie must now recover lost position. If a puck hits square, it stays on the same angle as the goalie and, therefore, does not require a positional recovery. A puck that hits a non-square surface rebounds elsewhere resulting in the goalie's angle being lost. While the same holds true of a narrower butterfly, the off-square surface is shrunk in size (evident in Fig. 2B) resulting in fewer rebounds when compared to a wider butterfly.

The second geometric lesson relates to the puck's angle of access. Once we have described this we can tie these geometric issues together to further explain the exasperation of rebounds using an excessively wide butterfly position.

The best way to define "angle of access" is with an illustration. In Figure 3, we can see that as the puck

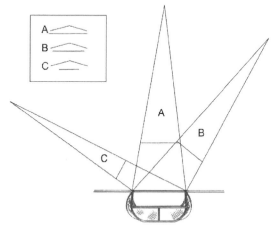

Figure 3 – Angle of Access Geometry

Three angles of access are illustrated to show the impact of the changing width of a shooter's angle. This means that a goalie's butterfly, too, can be adjusted in its width to be rebound-control efficient.

#3 – Narrow Your Butterfly

shifts position in the zone, different angles of access are created. The widest angle of access occurs when the puck is in the middle of the ice. As the puck shifts towards the boards, the angle of access shrinks as Figure 3 illustrates using angles A, B and C. Notice in the Fig. 3 inset that a wide-butterfly goalie uses the same butterfly width on all three angles and we can see that only in Angle A is the butterfly used efficiently. In other words, only here, does the butterfly not stretch beyond the "angle of access". This means that in both Fig. 3B and 3C the goalie is covering space outside the net. This creates a further inflammation of rebounds because pucks that are going harmlessly wide are being returned to scoring positions.

So, on two levels, the wide butterfly increases rebounds. The first is created by the width itself and the second is created by inefficient net coverage whereby the wide butterfly exceeds the "angle of access".

LEG MANEUVERABILITY

The issue of leg maneuverability is just as important an issue as the geometry noted above. The primary reasons that the blocker, glove and stick tend to have superior rebound control than the pads is because of their maneuverability. In the case of the glove, blocker or stick, the equipment in question can be taken to the puck and can be shifted and angled to coerce the puck in a desired direction. By narrowing an overly wide butterfly, the goalie reclaims some leg maneuverability. Given the size and bulk of the pads, they will never have the same control as the smaller pieces of equipment but, again, the objective is to not eliminate but reduce the frequency of dangerous rebounds.

Anytime the human anatomy is pushed to the limit of its range of motion all flexibility is lost. This makes sense. By placing ourselves at our extremes, it makes sense that we can no longer shift or move. Goaltenders have to make a choice between raw coverage (gained through a very wide butterfly) which provides preliminary benefits but limits long-term development or to focus on progressively building their game, with rebound control as a core development objective, throughout this building process. If the latter is one's desire then a versatile butterfly width is critical to long-term growth and success.

Goaltenders like Luongo, Brodeur, Kiprusoff and Hiller have opted for a narrower position when down which forces increased reactivity, improved reads and reduced rebounds. This isn't to say that a wide position does not work. There are also wider goalies, such as Fleury, Lundqvist, Ward and Backstrom who have developed superb games. These goalies, however, while using wider positions do not push their width to the extreme. In their cases, as with you, a balance must be struck between coverage and maneuverability. To be certain, every goalie is unique.

Coming back to the broader "narrower-butterfly" discussion, there are a host of other benefits associated with following this development path. To highlight some of these, they include:

- Improved rebound control
- Improved reactivity
- Reduced post interference
- Injury prevention
- Better read and anticipatory skills
- Enhanced peripheral response
- Improved depth of butterfly coverage (as opposed to width of coverage)

The value of "narrowing" your butterfly is a broad topic. It is something that exceeds the bounds of our focus – The 10 Secrets to Great Rebound Control – but is a focus that is worthy of an elite-level goaltender. It is also an important concept for younger goalies beginning to model their game.

#4
PUSH AND STEER - DON'T KICK

To further our discussion concerning rebound control with the pads, we shift our focus away from the raw benefits of a narrower butterfly and now look at some of the indirect benefits. The first is a concept we have coined "push and steer". The ability to push-and-steer is directly tied to a narrowing of the butterfly due to the available leg-maneuverability raised in the last chapter.

The ability to push-and-steer the puck with the leg pad is a primary method of controlling rebounds on the pads. Many goalies kick with the toes causing inflamed rebounds. Luongo highlights the push move in this photo and turns this puck to the corner.

Most goalies tend to kick with their toes. It is the most natural reaction to a puck. Like many things with the pads, this tends to increase rebounds not reduce them. Let's look at a butterfly and see what this common kicking reaction causes.

In Figure 1, we see a goalie's base butterfly. It is wide as indicated by the relatively close proximity of the ankles to the knee plane. The solid line indicates the natural path of the puck if it were to hit a static pad. This is easily determined with basic geometric functions. The dotted line is the new rebound path due to the kicking motion of the toe. This inflamed rebound puts the goaltender at greater risk.

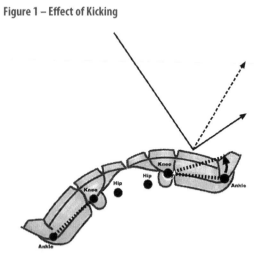

Figure 1 – Effect of Kicking

A goalie's natural tendency is to kick at pucks. This kicking motion with the toe, seen here, increases the volume and danger of rebounds off the pads.

The answer to this problem is to develop a more intuitive reaction – what we call "push and steer". Let's define this concept.

Think of the leg joints:

1. Hip
2. Knee
3. Ankle

"Pushing and steering" engages different joints than the more common "kicking" motion. The "kick" is a knee-driven move where the lower portion of the leg reacts by rotating out towards the oncoming puck (as indicated in Figure 1). In the case of push and steer, it is primarily the hips and, secondly, the ankles that are used. The knee, actually, maintains a more static position relative to the other joints.

This keeps the shin portion of the pad on a narrowed and more effective plane relative to the puck's trajectory. If we think about the goalie's leg pad, it is made up of three distinct sections:

1. At the top – the thigh rise
2. In the middle – the shin
3. At the bottom – the scoop

These segments are illustrated in Figure 2. They are important for this discussion because they help us describe the concept of "push and steer".

While the "kick" creates an amplified rebound effect by causing the angles of the scoop and the shin to direct pucks aggressively back into scoring positions, the "push and steer" has a more favorable result.

In Figure 3, we illustrate the basic notion of the "push". It involves an outward adjustment of the pad keeping the shin on a static angle relative to the puck. You'll

Figure 2 – Leg Pad Construction

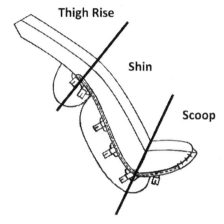

The goalie's leg pad has three distinct sections: thigh rise, shin and scoop. These sections help us explain the push and steer.

Figure 3 – The Push

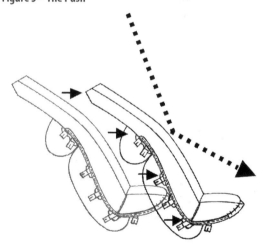

The push-and-steer movement is a parallel move by the pad. By parallel, we mean that the pad shifts laterally towards the puck on a similar angle as the original pad position (as indicated here).

notice that the initial position of the shin and adjusted position (i.e. post "push") are parallel, or near parallel, to one another. The affect of this pushing of the leg position outward is to push the puck rapidly in an outward direction relative to the net.

In Figure 4, we can see different angles and the effect of the push and the resulting puck position. This, again, is a simple geometric exercise.

As the pad moves outward in a "push" manner, the puck redirects in an altered but similar direction, in this case to the goalie's right side. There are two important benefits to this altered direction:

1. The puck is not altered significantly and, therefore, the pace of the altered puck remains high which handcuffs an offensive player
2. The puck's direction is altered or massaged away from the net but not severely and, therefore, tends to "steer" to the corners

Figure 4 – Effect of Pushing and Steering

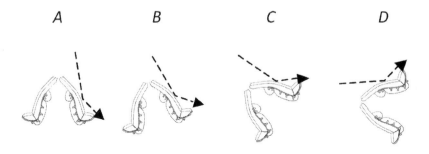

Using the push-and-steer technique, goalies dramatically reduce inflamed rebounds. It is only on severe angle shots where a push might cause the rebound to move into a dangerous position but, even in this case, the astute goaltender that uses a narrower / versatile butterfly will allow this "wide" puck to drift harmlessly by.

In Figure 4, we can see that only on a severe shot (Fig. 4D) does a "push" result in an inflamed rebound. In all other examples, the geometry of a "push and steer" results in the puck moving sharply away to non-threatening areas of the ice.

Learning to "push and steer" takes time and patience as our natural reaction is to "kick".

The three simple self-development drills (described at the end of the chapter) will help condition your body and leg joints to bring the push-and-steer skill into your game. As you do these drills, you need to consciously begin to apply the push-and-steer method in practice. There are countless shot opportunities to work on this rebound-control strategy and the reward of implementing this in your game is clear. You will be one of the few goalies, today, that can truly control pucks off of your pads. This is a complex area of rebound control. There are four secrets offered in this handbook to assist your rebound control with the pads:

1. Narrowing of the butterfly
2. Push and steer
3. Increased stick usage
4. Understanding square saves and geometry

As you implement these skills, your puck control will take off and your performance success will follow suit.

SELF-DEVELOPMENT DRILL PROGRESSION

PUSH-AND-STEER STRETCH

While down in your butterfly extend your right pad outward, parallel to the initial pad angle. Seek to stretch your groin during this process and hold the stretch for 10 seconds. Repeat to the other side. Do 3 repetitions to each side.

STATIC DOWN PUSH

While in your butterfly, quickly extend your right pad laterally in a push fashion. Once you reach the extent of your push flexibility recover the right pad back to your base butterfly. Repeat on the other side. With a short break between each one repeat this 10 times to each side, alternating sides.

DROP AND PUSH

Start in your stance. When ready, drop down to your butterfly and as your pads hit the ice, extend your right pad laterally in a push fashion. Recover this leg back to your base butterfly position and recover to your stance. Repeat to the left side. Do 10 reps to each side, alternating sides.

DRILL VARIATION

These two final drills can also be done with a coach shooting from the high slot (top of the circle distance from the net). In the first case, the goalies starts in the butterfly and the coach fires a puck along the ice to the right pad so that it can be pushed and steered to the corner. Do 10 reps to the right pad and then repeat to the left pad. The Drop and Push drill can be done with pucks in the same manner. Shots must be gapped properly so that the goalie can recover effectively before the next repetition.

#5
HAVE A STICK-TO-PUCK MENTALITY

Perhaps the most obvious way to control pucks around the pads, but the least utilized, is with the stick. In fact, traditionally, the stick was always used extensively for rebound-control purposes but as butterfly goaltending has become the norm, the stick has taken a backseat to the goalie's pads. Yet the stick is an excellent rebound-control tool while the pads are, generally, a poor rebound-control tool. So, as crazy as it seems, many goalies have swapped the very best rebound-control tool for the weakest.

Low shots are stick saves. This is an important mentality and one that can have a dramatic impact on reducing rebounds off the pads. Here, Roberto uses his stick to turn a puck aside. Unlike the pads, the stick is highly manipulative which helps direct pucks away from danger.

The 10 Secrets to Great Rebound Control

The objective of this chapter is to get goalies to recognize that the stick can be easily integrated to support the butterfly approach. Indeed, the stick should never have been discarded due to its versatility and maneuverability. It is a powerful tool across all bounds of a goalie's game with particular use to manage rebounds.

There are four important methods of controlling pucks with the stick:

1) Rotating pucks to the corner
2) Rotating pucks over the glass
3) Redirecting pucks to the corner that are at the five hole
4) Controlling and retaining pucks at the body

From an advanced perspective, another important element of stick control is the ability to raise the stick blade and position the blade or paddle to pick up further saves on elevated shots to the blocker side. This requires superior hand-eye coordination and lots of practice to develop. We'll start with the basics of stick control before discussing this more advanced aspect.

Basic stick control involves shots on the ice. Here, we are encouraging a near universal "stick-to-puck" mentality on these low shots. Goaltenders have evolved into more of a "pad-to-puck" approach as the butterfly has become more prevalent and has become the universal development philosophy of goalie coaches. It is important for coaches and goalies alike to not forget the benefits of historical approaches as we continue to evolve the position. Having a "stick-to-puck" mentality will help resurrect good rebound control while, at the same time, support the butterfly approach. We always want to add to the position as we evolve without subtracting.

As we think about having a "stick-to-puck" mentality, we are talking about the stick operating out in front of the butterfly position to intercept these pucks before they get to the pads. Notice the goalie is still using the butterfly position but the stick, with its added maneuverability, is managing the save and rebound with the butterfly supporting. Start with shots along the ice. These are the most obvious pucks that can be controlled with the stick and then one can graduate to more advanced, elevated shots.

When thinking about developing a "stick-to-puck" mentality, there is one time when the stick should not be used on low shots. This is when there is traffic and there is a deflection threat. In this case, it is important that the stick cover the five hole so that pucks don't get redirected back through as the goalie extends for a save. These cases should remain pad saves.

Before examining rebound-control support with the stick, we must start with strong stick basics. Remember, rebound control does not exist without proper fundamentals.

The basis of good stick use hinges on six key fundamentals:

1. **GAP** – means that the blade is positioned an appropriate distance from the toes of the skates.
2. **ANGLE** – refers to the angle of the blade, in relation to the ice.
3. **SQUARE** – refers to a square position relative to the puck.
4. **CENTERED** – means that the stick is primarily located in the center of the goaltender's stance.
5. **FLAT** – means that the blade is flat on the ice.
6. **FIRM** – means that the stick is held with a firm grip.

These are stick basics. Of course, there are many skills and tactics used in goaltending including adjustments to stance that can affect stick position. These adjustments are usually made during a shot-preparation mode (e.g. a relaxed stance to increase the size of a goalie's presentation). The basics listed here are save fundamentals and are the attributes of the stick just prior to a save.

Let's now look at the technical aspects of each stick skill as it relates to rebound control. This is a technically more intensive part of the book so take your time to understand the concepts.

ROTATING PUCKS TO THE CORNER

<u>The Initial Gap</u> – The most important puck-control role for the goaltender's stick is to rotate pucks to the corner. To accomplish this objective, the goaltender must start with a proper stick gap. This gap will change from goaltender to goaltender but should be approximately 18 inches. In other words, the stick will be placed 18 inches out in front of the skate position.

This gap is crucial for puck control and is shown in Figure 1. You'll notice that in addition to the gap the blade is angled. As we will see, this, too, can assist in puck control.

Figure 1 – Stick Gap

The stick gap should be approximately 18 inches and is used to assist in rotating pucks to the corner or over the glass.

Maintaining Gap

– The gap must be maintained regardless of a stance position or a down position. Many goaltenders, when they go down, lose their stick gap. The problem with a loss of gap is that it places the stick too close to the pad position and conforms the stick on the same angle as the pad causing the very rebound the goalie is trying to prevent.

Figure 2 – Stick Gap Comparison When Down

In Fig. 2, you will see the stick gap maintained and then the stick gap diminished while in a down position. It is easy to see that when the stick gap is maintained, the potential exists for a natural cushioning

The ability to maintain the stick gap during save movements and positional adjustments is essential to good stick use. Here, the front image shows a correct stick gap maintained while the goalie goes down. Conversely, in the back figure, the stick has ended up closer to the pad position creating the risk of lost puck control.

of the puck. When the gap is diminished, the puck does not cushion naturally and the puck might careen back to an attacking position.

The problem here for many goaltenders is that when they go down their knees drop forward. When the knees drop forward (e.g. during a butterfly) the stick position does not compensate by adjusting outward. Instead it stays in the same position and ends up tight and conformed to the pads. The solution is to allow the stick to push outward as the drop occurs to help maintain the necessary gap.

<u>The Rotational Arc</u> – The final phase of the stick rotation is the arc drawn by the stick as the save is made. As this arc is drawn it maintains the required gap to ensure clearance for the puck as the stick is rotated.

Figure 3 – Rotational Arc

The arc is shown in aerial Figure 3. Notice that the arc is drawn well out in front of the body position. Not only does this provide necessary cushioning but also, depending on the angle of the stick blade, assists in rotating the puck over the glass.

The circular path drawn out in front of the goaltender, in this aerial view, shows the rotational arc required to consistently place pucks into the corner or over the glass.

So, a combination of initial gap, gap maintenance and proper rotational arc is all that is required to rotate pucks to the corner and lay the groundwork for angling pucks over the glass.

ROTATING PUCKS OVER THE GLASS

<u>Stick Angling</u> – Angling of the stick (as illustrated and noted back in Fig. 1) is the next micro skill to develop. To move the puck out of play when stopping the puck on the glove side, the stick's angle must be adjusted and combined with the rotational arc. As the stick draws around the arc

the blocker hand is dropped down. The dropping of the blocker hand creates a greater stick angle and, when held firmly, the combination of arc, stick angle and firmness will force the puck on the required upward trajectory.

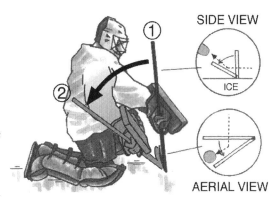

Figure 4 – Stick Angling

To get the puck over the glass, the goaltender will drop their blocker hand to get the desired angle on the stick. A combination of angle, arc and firmness will force the puck up over the glass. On the blocker side a dropping of the blocker hand is not possible so the original gap and angle must be such to give the puck a chance to elevate.

On the blocker side, it is not possible to drop the blocker hand in the above fashion. Therefore, the goalie needs to ensure that the proper angle and gap is achieved at the beginning of the arc to give the puck a chance to elevate over the glass. On this side, the stick naturally angles to support over-the-glass redirections.

WARNING: Be careful not to angle your stick blade too much or you may be the victim of directing the puck into your own net.

Firm Stick – The final element to successful rotations is the requirement to maintain a firm grip on the stick. A loosely held stick will always create an unpredictable puck response. A firmly held stick will force the puck to change trajectory in the desired manner.

REDIRECTING PUCKS THAT ARE AIMED AT THE BODY

One of the more difficult rebound-control challenges is a hard low shot at the goalie's five hole. Indeed, this is the first place where a point shot should be directed. For most goalies, this means an automatic rebound.

The more advanced goaltender can control this shot in one of two ways. The first is to accept the puck into their knee pads/stacks. This is a further benefit of a narrower butterfly (assuming the goalie's gear is configured properly). The second method involves a hard rotation to the corner using the stick.

It should be noted that it is impossible for the puck to be rotated over the glass in these cases. By taking this out of the equation and focusing on forceful rotations to the corner, the goalie has a better chance to eliminate these rebounds using the stick.

The ability to direct hard, on-ice shots coming at the goalie to the corner follows a similar progression as described in stick rotations with a couple of small exceptions.

First, there is no arc associated with this move nor is there stick angle to create elevation. So, the emphasis is placed on three key variables –firmness, elimination of angle and proper rotation.

Firm Stick – Turning these shots to the corner requires strength. A loosely held stick will create a partial cushion causing the puck to remain dangerously in the slot. It is the firmness of the stick that drives the puck quickly to the corner.

Stick Angle and Gap Eliminated – With the puck coming at the goaltender, the gap can be reduced. This reduction is often achieved simply by dropping into the butterfly with the knees forward in behind the stick. This reduction in gap helps to eliminate the upward angle of the stick. Now, the goalie has a firm and upright stick position.

Stick Rotated – Instead of arcing and angling the stick up, the goalie simply rotates the stick blade, using the hand

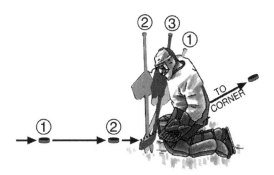

Figure 5 – Managing Pucks at the Body – Hard Rotations

In this illustration, we show both the reduced gap (1) necessary to increase the strength of the stick position, the removal of the stick angle (2) and the stick rotation (3) to coerce the puck in the desired direction.

and wrist, to move the puck in the desired direction. By creating a firm, perpendicular and rotated stick blade, the puck will careen to the corner.

Figure 5 (on the previous page) shows these elements in a combined view using numbers to illustrate the sequence of events.

CONTROLLING AND RETAINING PUCKS AT THE BODY

The final rebound control technique using the stick is to maintain control of the puck at the body. This is most often used when the puck is coming at slower speeds.

In this case the number of variables required to accomplish the task is reduced further. Now, only stick gap and firmness play roles.

Stick Gap and Firmness – Many individuals suggest that the goaltender should cushion a puck in order to control it at their body. However, this is exactly opposite to what should happen. By artificially cushioning a puck, the goaltender eliminates the gap which is required to control the puck at the body. By maintaining a proper stick gap and holding the stick firm, the velocity of the puck will create its own cushioning relationship with the stick blade. This is called a natural cushion.

Imagine a moving object hitting a stationary, firm but moveable object.

Figure 6 – Retaining Pucks at the Body

FIRM STICK

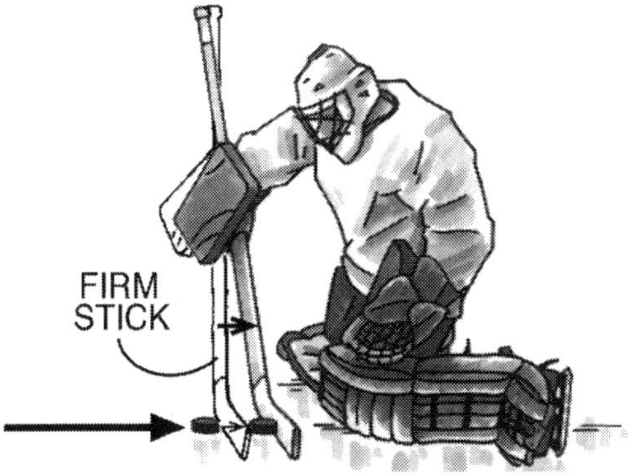

While in one's stance or down, the stick has a natural angle to its blade as shown in Fig. 1 earlier. When attempting to control the puck at the body position, the stick must be adjusted into a more upright blade position as shown here. Along with proper gap, this will create a natural cushion and help ensure the puck does not flip up or bounce right or left.

As the moving object hits the stationary object, the stationary object will be moved backwards. If this stationary object is firm it will slow the moving object down. As the moving object slows, the resisting object will require less force to slow the moving object. Finally, the two objects will stop moving altogether.

With no opposing movement from either object, in this case the puck and stick, the puck will remain on the stick. This is the natural cushioning effect created by preserving the gap between stick and pads (or skates) and maintaining a firm stick position.

Upright Stick with No Rotation – The last point to make on controlling the puck at the body is that the stick must maintain a square position to the approaching puck and cannot be angled upward nor rotated towards a corner. This will ensure that the puck is not coaxed in a direction and will stay on the stick. To accomplish this neutral stick position, the blocker hand must be pushed outward slightly (as in Fig. 5 number 2). This is done to eliminate the natural stick angle which is found in the goaltender's basic stance or basic down moves. Figure 6 (on the previous page) shows this natural stick angle as well as the adjusted neutral stick position.

ADVANCED "STICK-TO-PUCK" SKILLS

The advanced skill associated with developing a comprehensive "stick-to-puck" capability is to have the stick blade or paddle meet elevated pucks out in front of the pads, or even above the pads. There is not a skill progression with this capacity. Instead, this is very much a hand-eye coordination issue.

As the goalie tracks the puck visually, one who has developed a stick-to-puck mentality will elevate and draw the blade or paddle laterally across the face of the pad to meet the lifted puck.

The best way to achieve this skill, outside of natural hand-eye coordination, is to practice drawing the stick to elevated pucks in some warm-up drills. Often in these drills, a goalie can stand up more as they warm up and this is a great opportunity to practice this. As your warm-up progresses begin going down and using the blade/paddle to meet elevated pucks.

This skill is particularly useful on shots to the goalie's blocker side. This is great news. All goalies have a weakness to this side of the body due to the dual role that the blocker hand plays (i.e. controlling the blocker and also the stick). This is why goalies get beat over-the-pad blocker side. A goalie that has the ability to use the stick to meet these elevated pucks can diminish this deficiency.

To conclude this chapter, combining a narrower butterfly width with push-and-steer capabilities and increased stick use, goalies can finally begin to re-establish the complex area of puck control on the pads. Next up, we will put the finishing touches on the various methods of improving rebound control in the lower-body area. The avid goalie will seek to make all these improvements and when achieved will have a vast competitive advantage over their peer group.

#6

UNDERSTAND THE POWER OF SQUARE SAVES AND GEOMETRY

Geometry is fundamental to good rebound control and for good reason. Rebounds are pucks that have escaped a goaltender's possession and have redirected to a different scoring position. The redirection is caused by the puck hitting "a face" of the goaltender's gear. It is the contact of the puck with this "gear face" that determines the path and position of the rebounded puck.

Figure 1 highlights a simple geometric relationship between a moving object colliding with a plane. You'll recall this image from Chapter 3 – Narrow Your Butterfly. As stated at that time and re-affirmed here, the resulting rebound is a geometric reality.

When we think about rebound control, there are four basic options:

1. Retain
2. To the corner/ over the glass
3. Square to current position
4. Off square to current position

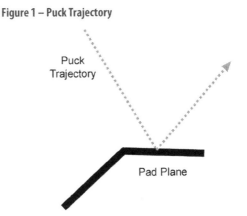

Figure 1 – Puck Trajectory

When a moving object collides with an unmovable plane, the object careens predictably in this fashion. In this case the moving object is traveling on an angular trajectory that equals X degrees relative to perpendicular and hits a stationary plane that is angled at Y degrees. The resulting new trajectory is easily calculated.

45

The 10 Secrets to Great Rebound Control

Luongo attempts to front as many pucks as possible with square surfaces. By reducing the number of off-square surfaces, he is able to keep more pucks in front him which improves his retention and also his positioning on subsequent shots.

As we consider our rebound-control objectives, it is imperative that we understand this ranking. Generally, this list is ranked from best result to least desirable result.

Ideally, goalies retain pucks. The rationale for this is simple. If you possess the puck then you control the game. With retention, you get to determine the next course of events. Perhaps, your team needs a whistle to get "fresh legs" on the ice. Perhaps, it's late in a period, with mere seconds to go, and you don't want a defensive-zone faceoff. Then, releasing a retained puck to allow the clock to wind down may make good sense. Nevertheless, you get to pick and, thus, you have control.

#6 – Understand the Power of Square Saves and Geometry

The second option, if a puck is not retained, is to put pucks into a non-scoring position. In general, this means behind the goal line to the corners. This is a logical option because it buys you and your team time to regroup or even establish possession of the loose puck. Sometimes, the "retention" objective and this second objective can swap places. For instance, when there is a lot of traffic, the goalie may prefer to direct the puck away from the net so a scramble does not ensue.

The third objective, square-to-current position is very important because rebounds are a reality of the position. Goaltenders want to improve their rebound control but the elimination of all rebounds is not possible. The ability to keep some of your pucks square to your current position (or, at least, on the same side of the ice) is an important skill. Think about this for a moment. If the puck stays in front of you, it remains in a scoring position but your positioning remains correct. Therefore, you are well positioned to make the next save. Clearly, this is favorable when compared to the alternative – a rebound that ends up "off square" to your current position. Figure 2, using Roberto, illustrates the power of a "square rebound".

Off-square rebounds are the most dangerous category because the puck has returned to a scoring position and your existing position is no longer valid. Therefore, a recovery of unknown urgency is required. The goalie that consistently pushes pucks into off-square

Figure 2 – Square Saves

A square save is defined as a save with a resulting rebound in which there is no, or little, positional adjustment required to manage the second shot.

scoring positions will ultimately fail regardless of recovery capabilities. Pucks move faster than bodies so pucks that are directed into threatening positions where the goalie's position is invalid will end up with more goals being scored. This is a plain fact. Figure 3 shows the danger of an "off-square" rebound.

Figure 3 – Off-Square Rebound

An off-square rebound is defined as a rebound in which a significant positional adjustment is required to manage the next shot.

We now know the rebound-control objectives; let's continue on our discussion of geometrics followed by further clarification of square saves.

SCORING POSITION GEOMETRY

Middle Positions

Generally speaking, middle positions (indicated by a goalie's angle being located inside the inner hash marks) are safer for a goaltender from a rebound-control perspective. This is due to the natural angles of the "gear faces" that tend to direct pucks into the corners. The "gear faces" are either square (i.e. torso and glove) to the oncoming puck or are angled, or can be angled, (i.e. blocker, stick and pads) in a manner that supports redirections to the corner.

A further benefit of middle positions is that recoveries require less rotation and shorter distances given that the rink has been "cut in half" by the middle position.

Angled Positions

Angled positions (indicated by a goalie's angle being located outside the inner hashmarks) are far more complex and require additional development on the following concepts:

1. Square saves
2. "Gear-face" manipulation
3. Dynamic rotation and recovery

Due to its importance, we will allocate the end this chapter to a strict focus on square saves. Again, this is where the goalie seeks to keep the puck in front of the current position to simplify secondary saves.

Manipulating the "gear face" (in particular, the far-side leg pad) is vital because this is the primary cause of difficult, off-square rebounds. The natural angle of the far-side pad will direct pucks not only into scoring positions but positions that are the farthest away and most dangerous to the goalie. These are "full width", off-square rebounds meaning they have been directed to the opposite-side of the ice. The ability to manipulate the leg pad to either make the rebound "more square" or, conversely, allow it to glance off the pad face and into the opposite corner are challenging skills.

These off-square rebounds that tend to occur from these angled positions require superb rotation and recovery mechanics. As we have already stated, you are not going to eliminate all rebounds and, therefore, your recovery skills must accommodate this fact. Remember, rotation comes before activation of the backside skate. This ensures that you are recovering, on the shortest path, to the new angle. This is especially important when pucks are directed to the opposite side of the ice. Chapter 8 – Reduce Post-Save Delay provides additional tutelage on this recovery topic.

CONCEPT OF SQUARE SAVES AND SQUARE SURFACES

Square saves in the context of geometry, means square surfaces. Again, this is about "gear faces". The more "gear faces" that are square to the oncoming puck, the squarer the save and, therefore, the more likely a square rebound. In this case, the validity of the current position remains. The primary "faces" that can be square include:

*   Torso
*   Thighs/pants
*   Stick

In both the first two cases, these should be naturally square to the oncoming puck because a goalies hips and shoulders should be square. The stick, on the other hand, can be manipulated to square, or even over square, to keep pucks on the same side of the ice.

In Figure 4, Roberto highlights the square nature of the torso and thighs. This is an excellent image that shows the squareness of his entire body.

Incidentally, the net is narrower and narrower as a shooter's angle becomes more severe. This is important because a goalie can develop a narrower butterfly to fit into this decreasing space and the square surfaces of the goalie can occupy a greater and greater proportion of this area. This is, in essence, the power of square surfaces, square saves and a narrower butterfly – we want to be square and geometrically efficient. Despite Luongo's 6'3" and 200+ pound frame, he exemplifies this efficiency of body positioning within these narrowing spaces.

Figure 4 – Square Torso and Thighs

Using a square torso and thighs is an advanced skill that can have a dominant effect on one's rebound-control capabilities. Here Roberto Luongo illustrates his ability to front the puck with a square body. He has, virtually, eliminated any plane that could cause an off-square rebound.

#7
EXCEL IN THE EASY AREAS

You have five means of making saves and, therefore, five ways to control rebounds:

1. Torso (body)
2. Stick
3. Glove
4. Blocker
5. Pads

Making sure simple saves are controlled effectively is critical to good rebound control. The glove, blocker, torso and stick represent save tools that have easy rebound-control characteristics. Like Roberto, seek to excel in these simpler areas to avoid sloppy rebounds and goals.

The 10 Secrets to Great Rebound Control

The first four methods listed are relatively easy from a rebound-control perspective. It's the fifth one, the pads, which poses a real complication for goalies of all ages and skill levels. So, our focus here is to examine the four easy ones and make sure that these are being handled properly and resulting in optimal rebound-control.

For each of the "easy" areas, here is a basic set of rules to help ensure that you are getting the maximum benefit from each one:

TORSO

The torso is the goalie's largest single area of coverage. This is important because it suggests that, for the well-positioned goaltender, the majority of shots are going to come into this region. The torso, then, plays a huge rebound-control role in our game.

In addition to being the biggest area of coverage, there are a few additional aspects of the torso that help make it such a prominent rebound-control tool.

The goalie's positional aim is to be centered, or on-angle, with the puck at all times. Since the body is our center it can occupy the majority of the puck-net relationship. This is true if the goalie has developed strong movement and positional fundamentals. Remember, the first of our "10 Secrets to Great Rebound Control" relating to fundamentals. A well-positioned goalie for many reasons will have superior rebound control and the relationship between a centered torso is one of them.

A further benefit is the general softness of the torso. This softness comes from two things: the goalie's chest protection and the ability to soften oncoming pucks. The notion of cushioning is a logical method of slowing and retaining pucks and there is no better example of this than the body unit.

To conclude then, the body is big, centered and soft which, when used effectively, leads to excellent rebound-control.

The following list highlights the keys which are all clearly illustrated in this chapter's opening picture of Roberto which is revisited and cropped in Figure 1:

1. Be well positioned
2. "Accept" pucks into your coverage (see Chapter 9)
3. Use your glove hand to assist in retention
4. In the lower area of your torso and upper thighs, concave your body to create a cushion effect

STICK

Please review Chapter 5 – Have a Stick-to-Puck Mentality to recall the fundamentals of stick control. The stick and torso represent the two most effective rebound-control tools

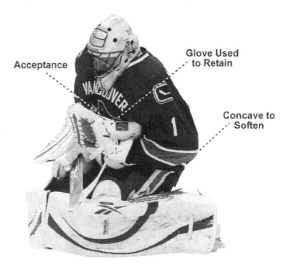

Figure 1 – Rebound Control and the Body

Well Positioned

The torso is the best control tool a goalie possesses. Along with the glove, the body allows the goalie to easily retain pucks, our number one objective, which allows us to control the pace and flow of the game. Here, we see the concepts of positioning, acceptance, glove use and concaving to control a puck on the body.

that you possess and should be prominently developed as such.

Using the stick for rebound control is a lost art. Too many goalies have foregone good stick use due to butterfly development. Pads have replaced the stick as the primary method of stopping shots on the ice. This is an incorrect development approach. Good stick use for save and rebound-control purposes is vital. In fact, pucks on the ice should be considered stick saves above all.

GLOVE

The glove catches pucks. Sure there are times when the glove catches a piece of the puck deflecting it back into play. However, the bulk of shots to the glove should be caught shots and, therefore, retention is easiest. Since the glove is mainly a catching mechanism, the dedicated goaltender should constantly seek to improve their hand-eye coordination to increase the volume of cleanly caught pucks.

BLOCKER

The blocker is a unique rebound-control tool. Like the glove and stick, it can easily be manipulated for puck-control purposes. Like the pads and stick, the blocker has a hard surface. This is contrary to the body and the glove. So, like all hard surfaces, the goalie tends to direct pucks with these tools as opposed to retain and cushion them as with the softer ones.

There are really two options with the blocker hand.

1. Turn the puck to the corner
2. Punch the puck past oncoming traffic

Punching the puck with the blocker is a viable rebound-control approach due to the closed nature of the forearm and hand.

The most common blocker response, however, is turning the puck to the corner. This requires a simple three-step process:

1. Lateral extension of the blocker arm to meet the puck
2. Turning the forearm to aim the blocker face at the corner, and
3. Cocking the wrist to direct the puck down and away from the net

Figure 2 – Rebound Control and the Blocker

A combination of extension, forearm rotation and a cocking of the wrist can make your blocker hand highly effective for rebound-control purposes.

 # 7 – Excel in the Easy Areas

Each of these elements is highlighted in our second cropped image of Roberto – Figure 2.

Punching the puck occurs when there is traffic, or a middle drive, and the goalie doesn't want to be as passive with the save. Here, the goalie extends outward in a punching motion to meet the puck ahead of the traffic. This moves the puck quickly and aggressively beyond the oncoming players. In this case, the arm extends out and forward with the same downward "cocking" motion to achieve the desired result. This tactic is used more sparingly and usually by bigger, stronger goaltenders.

To conclude, each of these rebound-control areas represents a beginner-to-intermediate skill level. One of the very best ways to further lock in superb rebound control in these "easy" areas is to take great pride in your rebound control during practice (see Chapter 10). Too often, these "easy" areas are taken for granted and poor habits are formed as we trivialize their simplicity. This is a dangerous course because sloppy practice habits will always creep into and affect in-game performance. Challenge yourself to stay sharp in these areas and excellent rebound control will soon improve your game.

The 10 Secrets to Great Rebound Control

#8
REDUCE POST-SAVE DELAY

As we have stated throughout these discussions, rebounds, to an extent, are inevitable. While the intent of this handbook is to help you improve your ability to control rebounds, it would be remiss for us to not discuss

Great visual attachment and a standardized post-save response allow Luongo to quickly reposition on rebounding pucks. Here he uses his stick smartly (instead of his pads), remains visually attached and begins his rotation all in one fluid movement.

how to actually handle rebounds that do occur.

Hockey is too unpredictable and too dynamic to eliminate all rebounds. Your objective should be to:

a) Eliminate as many rebounds as possible
b) Develop superb recovery skills to have greater success on those pucks that do get away from you

Hockey is all about time and space. Therefore, the goalie's ability to recover quickly is the key. The puck moves swiftly from position to position and we have to be able to match this pace from a positional perspective. If a puck deflects off our pad eighteen feet back into the slot, this might require an adjustment in position of four feet. We must cover the four-foot positional adjustment in the same amount of time it takes the puck to travel its eighteen feet out and then eighteen feet back to the net. This is called "positionally matching the puck's pace".

Good mechanics are vital to recovery skills and these skills include some of the things that you already know:

- Early eyes
- Proper rotation
- Activation of the backside skate
- Proper loading and gathering
- Lateral adjustment by way of any of the five lateral methods (T-push, shuffle, butterfly slide, backside push or knee shuffle)

These mechanics are not covered here but there is plenty of material describing these lateral skills. The main focus here is the reduction, bordering on eliminating, post-save delay. There are two primary concepts that can help reduce this delay:

1) Visual Attachment
2) Standardization of Post-Save Response

VISUAL ATTACHMENT

Simply stated – visual attachment is the key to the amount of delay in a goalie's game.

Why?

58

Well, this is an extremely straight forward concept.

If we don't know the location of the puck, it is impossible to move to the next position. Many goaltenders lose visual connection with the puck due to poor visual habits, which destroys their recovery pace.

As a goaltender visually searches to reconnect with a puck, movement and recovery are stalled and the correct directional move is delayed. To be certain, the opposition is not going to wait for this stalled goalie.

The visual sequence of goaltending as an attack develops is:

1) Early survey of the ice
2) Ongoing awareness (both #1 and #2 allow the goalie to understand the attack options which, in turn, helps fuel anticipatory skills)
3) Increasing visual focus on the puck carrier determining his intent
4) When a shot is taken, the goalie visually tracks the puck through the save and beyond (notice there is no disconnect)
5) Depending on the urgency of the subsequent play, the goalie recovers quickly due to the urgency of a second shot and/or the visual sequence begins again

As an aside, if the puck carrier passes the puck then the goalie's visual sequence includes early eyes on the new location of the puck. This is important because a rebound, in many ways, is like a pass. It shifts the puck from one position to another position on the ice. Therefore, the concept of visual attachment is closely linked to "early eyes". Notice that with a clear understanding of the puck's next position, the goalie has the information necessary to recover to the right spot.

We have used the same image (see Figure 1 on the next page) as was used earlier in the book relating to off-square rebounds to highlight the importance and concept of visual attachment. While this rebound is clearly dangerous, the fact that the goalie sees the puck means that they can initiate some kind of recovery response.

STANDARDIZATION OF POST-SAVE RESPONSE

The second important element of reducing delay is the concept of standardization. When a human has multiple choices or responses in a given situation, there is a decision-making process. Decisions take time and time, in goaltending terms, means delay and delay means goals.

Think about this in an exaggerated context.

You are doing a multiple-choice question with five answers ranging from (a) through (e). You read the question and then examine each answer. After contemplating the question and the potential answers a decision is made some time later.

Figure 1 – Visual Attachment

While this is an off-square rebound, the goalie does maintain visual connection with it and immediately understands the recovery requirement necessary to respond.

Let's now carry this exaggerated example one step further. Let's say on another test lies the very same question except in this case, the only choice is (a). Now, with only one option there is no contemplation required to respond. The response is immediate.

Let's translate to goaltending.

A goaltender makes a save with their right leg pad and pushes the puck to the right side of the ice. The goalie is visually attached and sees the puck's new location and instinctively formulates the necessary positional target. Now this particular goaltender, due to sub-par mechanics, uses one of any number of recovery processes:

a) Recover back to the feet using frontside leg and skate
b) Recover back to the feet using backside leg and skate but without rotation
c) Recover back to the feet using backside leg and skate but with rotation
d) Recover staying down using backside leg and skate after rotation
e) Dive across

Since this goalie has five different responses to the rebound, they must formulate which is the correct response. Just like our multiple-choice question, it takes time to process. This time, in a fast and dynamic event like hockey, may be brief but goaltending and hockey are all about time and space. This delayed goalie will either get scored upon or will complicate the second save due to the time lapse.

Now, let's consider the concept of standardization in response to a rebound. To standardize means to execute a single method of recovery. We have already listed it at the outset of this chapter. Here it is again:

- Early eyes / visual attachment
- Proper rotation
- Activation of the backside skate
- Proper loading and gathering

Notice that the final item from the previous list, the move into position, has been removed. The reason for this is that the goalie may or may not want to recover to the feet. There are times that a "down" recovery makes sense and, likewise, times when an "up" recovery makes sense. With this said though, the standardized response of early eyes, proper rotation, activation of the backside foot, and proper loading and gathering can be a goalie's singular, standardized response thus eliminating the time delay required for contemplation. This is like the exam question posed earlier in which there was only an (a) response. The answer/recovery can be immediate.

Figure 2 highlights the completion of the standardized

Figure 2 – Standardized Response

The goalie, in this off-square rebound scenario, has just completed the standardized response which includes: (1) early eyes, (2) proper rotation, (3) activation of the backside foot and (4) proper loading and gathering to ensure a strong and efficient lateral move to the new position.

response. In our fictional goalie's case, a choice between a down or up recovery is made at this juncture based upon the remaining time to respond.

In summary, it is our eyes through visual attachment that tell us what our next positional target is and it is the standardizing of our recovery process that reduces delay in our response. Combining these two powerful concepts will dramatically increase your recovery pace.

IMPORTANCE OF MULTI-TASKING

As a final comment, the goalie that builds strong visual attachment and standardized recovery will begin to achieve another time-saving skill. This is the ability to multi-task while recovering. As a goalie's eyes stay with the puck, through the save process, the goalie's recovery process initiates. As it continues, the goalie is able to begin formulating their strategy relative to the pending shot. This is all occurring at the same time and it is this multi-tasking goalie that becomes more fluid and quick to recover lost position. The objective is to have smooth, dynamic and rapid recovery all while reading and anticipating the unfolding threat.

#9
ACCEPT THE PUCK

Earlier we spoke about "Excel in the Easy Areas" where we dealt briefly with body fundamentals. Let's take a closer look because the torso is the goalie's largest area of coverage, is on angle and is a superb puck-control tool. The closer examination offered here will help you stop and retain more pucks in this area.

We have coined this chapter "accept the puck" and for good reason. Many goalies incorrectly turn body saves into glove saves. This occurs

The first lesson when using the body to control shots is to "accept the puck". Avoiding interference from the gloves, Roberto accepts the puck in his body unit and uses his gloves to help retain it with traffic on the doorstep.

for some goalies out of the natural defense mechanism of protecting the body through catching and deflecting. Of course, today, the goalie's torso is very well protected and it is this protection that also helps with puck control – if used effectively.

So, when we say "accept the puck", we are being very literal. Allow the puck to come into the body without interference from the hands or arms. This isn't to say that the hands shouldn't be involved to help retain the puck but the puck must first come through to the body unit.

A thorough review of body fundamentals will unveil the idea of "acceptance".

Remember that the torso is only effective if the goaltender is on-angle and in an effective depth position. It is this positional combination that places the goalie's body in that dominant position in which it fills the majority of the puck-net relationship.

Beyond the positional aspect, body cradling represents the mechanism by which the torso controls rebounds. In our Honorable Mention List at the end of the book, you'll find another body concept that further supports rebound control and further increases the use of the torso. This is the concept of center shifting.

Body cradles are the ability to accept the puck into the body and to then cradle the puck with the glove hand or through concaving to retain possession.

When cradling the puck there are five main development points:

1. The puck should be allowed to come into the body - i.e. accept the puck
2. The glove is brought under and into the body to seal the puck
3. The blocker remains wide to maximize the width of the goalie's coverage
4. Depending on the height of the shot, the body may concave itself to create a further cushion for the puck

Here's a detailed breakdown:

PUCK ALLOWED TO COME INTO BODY COVERAGE

The most important development point for goaltenders is to allow the puck to come to the body. As we stated earlier, goalies often attempt to make saves with their glove and/or blocker when the body should have been used. Using gloves to intervene on body saves is an unnecessary and inconsistent approach to puck control. Furthermore, it should not be necessary if proper protective gear is worn.

When one attempts to catch a puck coming at the body, the glove arm must remain forearm-open to the shot. This is a distorted and awkward body position, which makes it an inconsistent approach.

Likewise, the blocker has its limitations when brought in front of the body. In the blocker's case, it is not a distorted arm position that is the reason for concern but rather, the hard surface of the blocker which creates inconsistent and erratic redirections.

Another point supporting acceptance by the body relates to coverage. Hands being brought in front of the torso represent "double coverage". In other words, the hands and arms are now placed in front of the body covering the very space that the body has already taken care of. As a result, the goalie loses width. Goalies want to be square and wide within

Figure 1 – Body Cradle Sequence

Point 1 (Puck Acceptance) – The most difficult aspect of body cradling for most goaltenders is simply allowing themselves to use their body. In most cases, goalies instinctively try to use their glove and blocker to control the shot. Use of the body, with a glove cradling, after acceptance, is a superior approach.

Point 2 (Glove Cradle) – The cradling of the puck is achieved by bringing the glove under and into the body. As the glove comes to the body, the puck should be sealed. Make sure the glove-side elbow remains compact to the body.

Point 3 (Sealing of Puck) – The sealing of the puck is the final phase in which the glove comes into the body in a manner that does not allow the puck to drop back into play.

the space, especially in the upper body area.

The beauty of the body is it is impenetrable, big and soft. A goalie couldn't ask for three more effective puck-stopping, puck-controlling and puck-retaining characteristics. It makes sense then that the goalie would use this area as frequently as possible.

Figure 1 (shown on the previous page), shows a 3-point execution by a patient goaltender keeping their gloves wide in order to accept the puck into the body coverage.

GLOVE CRADLE – UNDER AND IN MOVEMENT

In some cases, the glove may not be necessary for rebound control when the puck enters the body coverage. This is often true when the body is concaved as described in detail below. However, there are times when the glove is an essential conclusion to controlling the shot on the body. The most common shots in which this is required are higher shots on the torso (as illustrated in Fig. 1).

When the glove is required, the procedure is to bring it from below and up as required to seal the puck on the body. The timing of this move is crucial. If early, the glove may interfere with the original puck trajectory. If late, the control of the puck may be lost and the puck may bounce off the harder area of the upper torso.

Another aspect of this glove mechanism relates to the elbow. In particular, on shots coming into the body region, the goaltender's coverage objectives are twofold – compact and wide. On the glove side, while width cannot be maintained if the glove is used, the compactness objective is achieved by maintaining a tight elbow-to-body position (this can be seen on the glove side in Fig. 2).

BLOCKER REMAINS WIDE

Again, the goalie's coverage objectives are compact and wide. On the glove side (of the body) this was partially achieved by maintaining the close elbow position. The blocker side can be even wider. Since the blocker does not need to play a role in the body cradle, it can remain in an adjacent position at the goalie's side.

Figure 2 – Wide and Compact Blocker

Since the blocker plays no role in a body cradle, it remains compact at the goaltender's side. This helps broaden the width of the goalie's coverage and allows the stick to remain in a stronger center-body position. On the left side we show a correct blocker hand so you can compare it to the incorrect example on the right.

This provides additional width to the goalie's coverage (especially important in traffic) and is shown in Figure 2.

CONCAVING OF BODY

Figure 3 – Body Concaving

On a final cradle/acceptance note, depending on the height of the shot, the goaltender may want to cushion the puck further by dropping their upper body forward slightly. What is really happening is that the body's trunk region (i.e. abdominals) contracts, concaving the upper body. This will have a further cushioning and enveloping effect on the puck. Figure 3 shows this completed move. This concaving move is equally evident in this chapter's opening photo of Roberto.

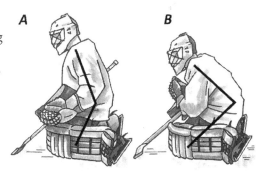

To further soften, cushion and envelope the puck, the goalie may elect, depending on the height of the shot, to concave their body by contracting their abdominal region. Fig. 3a shows the upright start position while Fig.3b shows the concave effect.

The 10 Secrets to Great Rebound Control

The "accepting of the puck" is not only extremely effective but a very simple concept and a very simple adaptation within the goalie's game. This is another great example of how rebound control can quickly be implemented into your game using simple and effective processes.

When you add up "The 10 Secrets to Great Rebound Control" along with our Honorable Mention items, you can very quickly advance your rebound control which, as stated frequently, has a direct correlation to improved performance.

#10
DEVELOP REBOUND-CONTROL PRIDE

Perhaps the single greatest word of rebound-control advice comes in this chapter. As is the case with the achievement of all developmental objectives, one's personal approach, care and attention to detail

As with anything, the volume of pride and care that is applied to a skill or habit the stronger the result. Having spent over half a decade working with Roberto in practice, the pride he demonstrates when handling rebounds transcends itself into exceptional rebound control in his game.

underscore the likelihood of fulfillment. Really this comes down to the pride in which you conduct yourself particularly during practice times.

We know from our first handbook (The 10 Quickest Ways to Improve Your Game) and from the demands of many coaches that our game habits are largely built in practice. This occurs for obvious reasons. First and foremost is the increased volume of repetitions in practice compared to a game. Here's a simple example:

Team Quality	Average Shots per Game	Gross Game Repetitions	Net Game Repetitions	Average Shots per Practice	Gross Practice Repetitions	Net Practice Repetitions
Excellent	18	90	68	200	1000	750
Good	25	125	94	200	1000	750
Average	32	160	120	200	1000	750
Poor	40	200	150	200	1000	750

Table Definitions:

Team Quality – This is the quality of the team from a performance perspective. We have all had experiences playing on very poor teams and also very strong teams. This impacts the volume and quality of shots against. For the purpose of this example, we did not change the ratio of repetitions based on team quality although there is an argument for this which would further inflame the example.

Average Shots per Game – This is the average number of shots the goaltender contends with during a game. In truth, for every shot against there is a likely a shot blocked or missed which also provides skill repetitions but we have ignored them to simplify the example.

Gross Game Repetitions – For every shot against, we are presuming there are five total skill repetitions – for example, the goalie may shuffle, maintain angle, make a save, visually track the puck and recover on a given shot. There are more micro skills involved than this but, again, for simplicity's sake, we are assuming a total of five skill repetitions per shot.

Net Game Repetitions – We assume that 25% of game shots are throw-away shots for technical-development purposes. This is due to the dynamic and unpredictable nature of the game. While the goalie gets plenty of benefit from these shots, from a battle and competitive standpoint, their mechanics inevitably break down in order to make these less-patterned saves.

Average Shots per Practice – This is the average number of shots the goaltender contends with during a team practice. This is the same definition as Average Shots/Game.

Gross Practice Repetitions – As we did for game shots, we are assuming there are five total skill repetitions (of varying types) on a given shot.

Net Practice Repetitions – As we did for game shots, we assume that 25% of practice shots are throw-away shots for technical-development purposes. In practices, however, this is due to poor quality shots due to drill structure, lackadaisical effort by teammates or some other force uncontrollable by the goalie.

#10 – Develop Rebound-Control Pride

So what does this table tell us?

The moral of this story is highlighted in the two gray columns. For many goalies, the volume of skill repetitions in practice is approximately 7X's greater than during games. This can become extreme based upon a goalie's ratio of practices to games as evidenced by our next table.

Goalie	Ratio of Practices to Games	Net Practice Repetitions	Net Game Repetitions
1	2:1	1500	120
2	3:1	2250	120
3	4:1	3000	120

We have assumed that each of our three goalies plays for an "average" team. Depending on their Practice-to-Game Ratio, the number of skill repetitions available in practice compared to games can rise to 25X's.

Let's correlate this back to our rebound-control discussion – remember that for each shot there are five skill repetitions. We break these down on average as follows:

	TOTAL SKILL REPETITIONS
PREPARATION	2
SAVE EXECUTION	1
POST SAVE (includes recovery and rebound control)	2

This means that 40% of our practice repetitions are related to rebound-control and/or recovery activities. The goaltender that has superb attention to detail and habits in these post-save skills will translate this to superior rebound control during games. It's that simple.

As a rule, then, goalies should not trivialize any rebound in practice. Careless puck control will creep into and infect your game. Since we know that the most common source of "grade A" scoring chances for the opposition occur from rebounds, we also know that this is the best source of performance improvement. Careless rebounds result in careless goals. It's simply a numbers game. If we push too many rebounds into scoring positions some of these will find their way into our net.

The 10 Secrets to Great Rebound Control

Too often in practice we get tired and the first thing that gets careless, in the face of fatigue, is the post-save. This is one of the main reasons the majority of goalies do not have good rebound control.

We have made this Chapter 10 because if you can take the other "9 Secrets to Great Rebound Control" and apply this high degree of pride and care to your practice habits, you will be shocked at how quickly your game is impacted. Do not underestimate what is being stated here. Do not do what the majority of readers do and say something like "Obviously, you need to have good practice habits" or some hybrid of this.

No. You need to recognize that Chapter 10 is the most important chapter in this handbook and the most important "Secret to Great Rebound Control" because without this level of pride and care, you can't truly develop the other nine improvements.

HONORABLE MENTION

We have identified our 10 Secrets to Great Rebound Control but we would be remiss to not mention these five additional essential tips and strategies. These additional five items carry significant weight. Indeed, it would be easy to suggest that this handbook should be characterized as the 15 Secrets to Great Rebound Control. So, don't forget these gems:

1. **<u>Learn to center shift</u>** – The torso is the goalie's single largest area of coverage and is, arguably, the best rebound-control area the goalie possesses. Therefore, anything that can increase torso use and put it in the face of an oncoming puck is going to provide a rebound-control benefit. The concept of center shifting is straightforward. It simply means that the center of one's body shifts towards the oncoming puck's trajectory. This ability to laterally shift into the puck increases torso use and, as a further benefit, reduces extension. When extension is reduced not only does this improve save success but makes recovery more efficient.

2. **<u>Don't react to wide pucks</u>** – This is really an argument for a versatile butterfly width. One of the most common rebounds results from a shot to the far-side pad. In fact, this is common because coaches specifically instruct their offense to follow this tact with a middle-drive attacker looking to pick up the rebounding puck. In truth, a lot of these bad-angle shots are actually going wide. A goalie that understands their positioning

and required coverage can reduce rebounds by simply not reacting to pucks that are directed wide. Very wide butterfly goalies that don't have versatility in their width are the biggest culprits of this mistake.

3. **React don't block** – Reacting to pucks is the very best way to control rebounds and for good reason. By definition, a reaction is specific to a shot. The goalie waits for the shot to be taken and then seeing the puck, reacts accordingly. Therefore, the save is custom made for that particular shot. Blocking, by definition, is establishing a large area of coverage within the space and then letting the puck hit this coverage. Notice that this is a general and not a specific response to the puck trajectory which is why it lacks the puck control of a true reaction. As a rule, you want to have a higher proportion of direct reactions as opposed to general blocks.

4. **Direct pucks away from scoring positions hard and fast** – Rebounds are a fact of hockey. This is why our objective is to reduce rebounds. Eliminating all rebounds is not possible. So, if a rebound is going to occur, we can use two tactics to help prevent the opposition from scoring. First, as indicated in Chapter 8, is to reduce post-save delay and have a dynamic and explosive recovery. The second tactic is to wear gear that supports hard and fast rebounds. This handcuffs the offensive player because of the puck's pace. Using hard gear to force hard redirections combined with explosive recovery skills will further improve your rebound success.

5. **Keep pucks on the same side of the ice** – This is similar to the concepts presented in Chapter 5 – Understand the Power of Geometry and Square Saves. The statement – keep pucks on the same side of the ice – is a simple, powerful statement to play by. It means that you want the puck to stay in front of you. As long as the puck is in front of you then you are in position. This makes it very difficult for the rebound to penetrate back through to the net.

CONCLUSION

We have provided you with The 10 Secrets to Great Rebound Control. However, the very best tip that we can give you is right here and supports the concept in Chapter 10. YOU need to take responsibility for your game and your improvement. Remember the following mantra and these improvements will take hold and your development and performance will take off:

You are your best goalie coach

When you embrace this mindset, your potential is truly unlimited because you have taken responsibility for your growth, development and performance. Goaltending coaches, like Leo and I, can help facilitate improvements in your game and can be partners in your growth but nobody can have the impact that you yourself can influence through pride in performance at all times.

So, take these 10 secrets and the five honorable-mentioned items and get after your rebound control. Watching goaltenders like Roberto Luongo, Marc-Andre Fleury and Cam Ward work on their game, one can easily see their level of commitment, attention to detail and, above all, the responsibility they take for their own growth as the ultimate keys for their success.

The 10 Secrets to Great Rebound Control

Waiting for others to develop your game is a sure-fire way to mediocrity. Ian Clark cannot be the catalyst. Leo Luongo cannot be the catalyst. As mentioned, we can be there and we can facilitate but we cannot direct your future success – only you can author that story.

Stay tuned for additional handbooks in The 10 Series.

Good luck in your goaltending and we wish you the very best as you challenge your game to the next level.

Ian Clark   Leo Luongo

BIOGRAPHIES

IAN CLARK

Ian Clark has been a NHL Goaltending Coach since 2001 when he joined the Florida Panthers. In July, 2002, he joined the Vancouver Canucks as Goaltending Consultant and remained with the organization through the 2009/10 hockey season. A former resident of Vancouver, Clark currently resides in Dallas, Texas and was the Founder of GDI-The Goaltender Development Institute. He was also the Editor-in-Chief of "From the Crease" and "The Goalie News", leading development publications for goaltenders of all ages and skill levels.

Clark has been a member of Team Canada's World Junior Championship coaching staff for four years and helped lead the team to two consecutive gold medals in 2005 and 2006. Recognized as one of the leading educators of the goaltending position, Clark's knowledge and innovative training has attracted high-performance goaltenders at the NHL, minor pro, major junior and NCAA levels.

Clark has worked with many of today's leading netminders including Roberto Luongo, Cam Ward, Marty Turco and Marc-Andre Fleury to name a few. Clark-trained goaltenders can be found in 21 of 30 NHL organizations.

LEO LUONGO

Leo joined GDI as a Regional Manager in 2007. He has studied under goaltending instructors François Allaire, Frantz Jean and GDI Founder Ian Clark, as well as his brother, NHL goaltender Roberto Luongo. Currently, Leo is a Goaltending Coach/Consultant in Montreal where, for more than 5 years, he has successfully developed goaltenders of all ages. He has provided instruction at many summer camps alongside François, Frantz Jean, Roberto and, separately, Ian Clark. Leo is also a member of Hockey Canada's National Goaltending Consultants Team.

As a goaltender, Leo played elite level hockey his entire career. He is currently the goalie coach for the Acadie Bathurst Titans in the QMJHL and is considered one of the top up-and-coming goalie coaches in the game.

NEXT IN THE 10 SERIES
The 10 Intangibles of the Great Goalies

The next in The 10 Series of handbooks on goaltending is *The 10 Intangibles of the Great Goalies.* The power of strong technique and explosive athleticism is clear in today's goaltending world. However, these tangible inputs only tell half the story of goaltending success and, for that matter, failure.

Forget about mechanics and athleticism. What really makes the great goalies great? Stay tuned for the next in The 10 Series of Goaltending Handbooks – *The 10 Intangibles of the Great Goalies.*

The 10 Intangibles of the Great Goalies

The intangibles of the position are those factors that one cannot develop through mere repetition. Repetition is a powerful concept when it comes to a goalie's mechanics or fitness capabilities but it doesn't carry the same weight when it comes to the mental/intangible realm of the position.

How, then, does a goalie develop key intangibles if there isn't a repetitive formula to follow?

Learning *The 10 Intangibles of the Great Goalies,* in the upcoming book by NHL Goaltending Coach Ian Clark and his contributing authors, will be a key step in this journey. Understand the power of self innovation, among other traits, that will drive your game up and off your current plateau. Most of all, combining continuous technical and athletic growth with advancement of these intangibles will, as do all handbooks in The 10 Series, help you stop more pucks.

NOTES

Made in the USA
San Bernardino, CA
13 August 2017